Domain

I0016016

Made Easy

Jim Stephens

Introduction

Buying a domain name is a relatively simple process, but it can be confusing managing them. There are a lot of options to consider, and there are hundreds of registrars to choose from.

There are several important decisions you'll need to make. It's not enough to simply register a domain from the first place you find. You need to choose the best possible domain for your website, buy from a registrar you can trust, and manage it effectively.

You'll also need to decide whether or not you want to use WHOIS protection, whether to park the domain, and how long to register it. Believe or not, these things do make a difference.

In this report, you're going to learn all of these things and more. You'll find out exactly how to register a domain and manage it correctly.

So let's get started

Choosing a Registrar

The first thing you need to do is decide which registrar you wish to use.

GoDaddy is a popular choice, but I don't recommend it. According to many people, they are prone to disabling domains even over false spam reports, and then charging a huge fee to reinstate the domain, even if you can prove you did nothing wrong.

NameCheap (http://www.namecheap.com) is a popular option. They have free WHOIS protection for the first year of each domain, and they have a coupon each month that lets you get a nice discount, making each domain less than $10.

I will use NameCheap as the example in this guide, because I consider it to be the best registrar. It is affordable, the support is good, and their interface is easy to use.

I don't recommend using the domain services of a hosting company. They will often hold your domain hostage and make it difficult to transfer it if you decide to leave their hosting. Always register your domain yourself, and always do it directly through a registrar.

Finding a Domain Name

Many people believe all the good domain names are taken. This isn't true.

While it's true that you aren't going to be able to pick up books.com or anything similar, there are still plenty of great domains available.

In order to choose the right domain for your purposes, you need to decide what you're going to use the domain for. There are two main classifications.

Keyword Domains

If you want to create a niche-based blog or website or you want to invest in a domain that you can sell for a profit later, you'll want to buy a keyword-based domain name.

You should look for domain names that have high-traffic keywords. If you wanted to make a site about Discount Golf Clubs, you would ideally want to get DiscountGolfClubs.com.

Keyword domains, especially for keywords that get significant numbers of searches, also have great resale value. You could buy a domain for $10 and flip it for hundreds, or even thousands.

Branding Domains

If you want to create a site that will be branded like Twitter or Flickr, you can be a little more creative. You'll want to get a one word domain (or two at most). But you can use creative spelling.

When buying a domain for

branding purposes:

1.   Look for a word that won't be too difficult to spell. Flickr is relatively easy to remember, but Fotograffi might not be. Too many letters are changed. People might not remember which ones are different from the original word. It should be memorable.

2.   Choose a word that fits your niche. For a site about golf, you might get something like Puttr.com, for example.

3.   Integrate your branding. Make sure you can craft a logo that will help people remember your domain name.

Warning: Do NOT search for domain names on any registrar until you are ready to buy! Some registrars make deals with speculators to provide recently searched names to them. They buy the domains and then charge a premium for them later.

Registering a Domain

Once it's time to register a domain, you need to keep a few things in mind.

First, don't use fake information during the registration process. You could get your domain taken away from you later, which would be a real shame if you've built significant traffic to it.

Second, you'll probably want to register all of your domains with the same registrar. It gets tedious having to worry about your domains at multiple registrars.

You'll also need to decide whether or not you want to use WHOIS protection, and how long to register the domain for.

WHOIS Protection

Many people automatically opt for WHOIS protection, but this isn't always the best option. Some SEO experts have suggested that Google and other search engines may penalize sizes who have their registration information protected.

Additionally, some customers may not trust you if you protect your information. This could result in lost sales.

However, if you are worried about people finding out what you're doing or coming to your home, you may wish to use WHOIS protection or at least give a P.O. box instead of a street address.

Registration Length

You can register your domain for only one year, or most registrars will allow you to register a domain for up to ten years at a time. If you can afford it, go for a longer registration period.

For one thing, you won't be at risk of accidentally forgetting to renew your domain. You'd be surprised how often this happens. You may not get the reminder email, and if you don't have it set up to automatically renew, you could lose the domain.

Another major reason to register for at least two years at a time is because some SEO experts believe Google may give a boost to sites with longer registrations. They believe Google may think a site is more trustworthy if it is registered longer, because spammers usually register for only a year, assuming they may get banned quickly, anyway.

Name Servers

In order to use your domain, you need to set up the name servers. This tells computers where to find your domain when someone tries to go there. It connects your domain with your web server.

I'm going to show you how to set up your name servers with NameCheap. You'll need your name servers from your hosting company. You may be able to find these in your control panel, or in the welcome email you got from them. If you can't find them, contact your hosting company and ask. You'll need two. They will look like this:

Log into NameCheap. Beside "Number of domains in your account", click "view". Then find the domain you want to modify and click it. In the menu

on the left, click
"Domain Name
Server Setup".

Click the selection field beside "Specify
Custom DNS Servers (Your own DNS
Servers). Then enter both DNS servers and
click "Save Changes". You're done!

Domain Forwarding

You may not always want to host a website or blog on your domain name.

You might want to use it to forward elsewhere. For example, article marketers often use domains to forward straight to their affiliate links.

It's very simple to set up domain forward with NameCheap, but you can only use it if you are using their default name servers. You'll have to switch them back to NameCheap's before you proceed.

Log into your account and select Manage Domains. Click the domain you want to forward and choose "All Host Records". In the "@" field, enter your domain name. In the "www" field, enter the URL you want to forward the domain to (for example, your affiliate link.) Be sure it says "URL Redirect" under "RECORD TYPE".

To transfer the name servers back to NameCheap, click your domain and select "Transfer DNS Back to Us" from the left menu. Then tick the boc beside "Transfer DNS to NameCheap Default DNS and click "Save Changes." Do this before you attempt to set up forwarding; otherwise, you won't have the option available.

Domain Parking

You can make money with your domain name when it's not in use by parking it. You won't make a lot unless your domain is visited very often, but it's better than nothing if you aren't currently using the domain, anyway.

As with forwarding, you can only park a page if you have changed your domain to NameCheap's default name servers. Once you have done that, go to "Manage Domains", click your domain, and select "Customize Parked Page". You can then change your parked page to whatever you want.

Keep in mind that you won't be able to add images to a parked page. You can only use text on it. But you can use various types of ads there. Just make sure they allow parking, because some companies (like Google AdSense) don't allow their ads to be displayed on websites with no content, like parked pages.

Parking your domain can help you make a little money while you decide what to do with a domain, or while it is under development.

Good luck!